The Inner Planets

Stuart Clark

www.heinemann.co.uk/library
Visit our website to find out more information about **Heinemann Library** books.

To order:
 Phone 44 (0) 1865 888066
 Send a fax to 44 (0) 1865 314091
 Visit the Heinemann Bookshop at www.heinemann.co.uk/library to browse our catalogue and order online.

First published in Great Britain by Heinemann Library, Halley Court, Jordan Hill, Oxford OX2 8EJ, part of Harcourt Education. Heinemann is a registered trademark of Harcourt Education Ltd.

Editorial: Nick Hunter and Catherine Clarke
Design: Jo Hinton-Malivoire and AMR
Picture Research: Maria Joannou
Production: Viv Hichens

Originated by Dot Gradations Ltd
Printed in Hong Kong, China by
Wing King Tong

ISBN 0 431 15453 8
06 05 04 03 02
10 9 8 7 6 5 4 3 2 1

British Library Cataloguing in Publication Data
Clark, Stuart
The inner planets. – (The universe)
523.4
A full catalogue record for this book is available from the British Library.

Acknowledgements
The publishers would like to thank the following for permission to reproduce photographs: Bettmann (Corbis) p. **14**; Calvin J. Hamilton p. **22**; Corbis (Stephanie Maze) p. **9**; Getty Images p. **29**; NASA pp. **24**, **26**; NASA / JPL / Caltech pp. **5**, **15**, **18**, **25**, **27**, **28**, NASA / JPL / Malin Space Science Systems pp. **19**, **20**; NASA / JPL / Northwestern University pp. **10**, **11**, **23**, NASA / Marshall Space Flight Centre p. **13**; NASA / National Space Science Data Centre p. **17**; NASA / Space Telescope Science Institute p. **21**; NASA / U.S. Geological Survey pp. **8**, **16**; Photo Researchers Inc. pp. **6** (John Foster); **7** (D. Van Ravensway; **12** (Chris Butler).

Cover photograph reproduced with permission of Photodisc.

Contents

Any words appearing in the text in bold, **like this**, are explained in the Glossary.

Are there other planets like Earth?

Humans have always wondered if there are any other **planets** like Earth. Thousands of years ago, the people of ancient Greece wrote down what they saw in the night sky. Most stars appear to move across the sky at the same speed. They make star patterns called **constellations**. The Greeks noticed five 'wandering stars'. They each moved across the sky at different speeds from the other stars. The Greeks called them *planetes*, which means wanderers. Now, we call them planets.

Studying the skies

Using telescopes, **astronomers** have discovered there are three more planets. This means that there are nine planets in total, including Earth. All of them follow paths around the Sun. These paths are called **orbits**.

The planets far away from the Sun are called the **outer planets**. They are very different from Earth. They are much larger than Earth and made mostly of gas. The planets near the Sun are called the **inner planets**. They are more like Earth. They are about the same size as Earth, or smaller, and are made mostly of rocks and metals.

Four inner planets

Mercury is the closest planet to the Sun. Venus comes next. Earth is the third planet from the Sun. The last inner planet is Mars. It is about 228 million kilometres from the Sun. That is about one and a half times further from the Sun than Earth. Then there is a large gap before Jupiter, which is the first outer planet.

What is between Mars and Jupiter?

Astronomers once thought that another inner planet must live in the space between Mars and Jupiter. In 1800, a group of astronomers called themselves the **celestial police** because they wanted to find the missing planet. Another astronomer, Giuseppe Piazzi thought he had found the missing world and beaten them to it. It was a big surprise because it was only 1023 kilometres across. That is much smaller than the other planets. Then the celestial police found another tiny world. Then they found another one, and another one! There is not one planet between Mars and Jupiter but a band of millions of tiny planets. They are called **asteroids**. Even today, astronomers are finding new ones.

Mars is nicknamed the 'red planet'. Like Earth it has a North and a South Pole. You can see the frozen North Pole in this picture.

Can you see the other inner planets?

You can see the inner planets in the night sky, if you know where to look. Two of them never move far away from the Sun because they are the planets closer to the Sun than Earth. These are Mercury and Venus.

The evening star

Venus is sometimes called the evening star because you can see it just after the Sun has set. It shines very brightly in the twilight sky. In fact, when Venus is in the sky, it shines brighter than any other star or planet. When Venus is on the other side of its orbit, however, it appears in the morning sky instead.

Mercury is harder to see than Venus because it stays even closer to the Sun. Also, it is not as bright as Venus. Mars is a red colour. It moves through the sky more slowly than Mercury or Venus because it is further from the Sun.

In this photograph, the planets Venus, Mars and Jupiter appear at sunset in the sky over Utah, USA.

Moving at different speeds

A year on Earth is 365 days. This is the time it takes our planet to travel around the Sun once. All the planets move around the Sun at different speeds. They also have different sized orbits. Mercury's is the smallest orbit and it is the fastest planet, too. It takes just 88 of our days to go around the Sun. Venus takes 225 days to travel through its orbit. Mars is the slowest of the inner planets and takes 687 days to go around the Sun.

This picture shows all nine of the planets in our solar system. Each planet goes round the Sun in its own orbit, at a different speed from the rest.

Each of the inner planets spins around too. It takes Earth 24 hours to spin around once on its **axis**. This gives us day and night. When one side of Earth is facing towards the Sun, it is daytime for that side of Earth. The opposite side of Earth points into space and it is night-time there. On Mercury, it takes 59 Earth days for the planet to spin around once. Venus is even longer – it takes 243 days to spin once on its axis. On Venus, a day is longer than a year. Mars's day is similar to Earth's. It spins once every 24 hours and 37 minutes.

Moons

Moons are objects that orbit planets. Two of the inner planets have moons travelling around them. Earth has one large moon, called the Moon. The Moon is only a little bit smaller than the planet Mercury. Mars has two tiny moons, called Phobos and Deimos. Neither Mercury nor Venus have moons.

This was one of the first photos taken of Mercury. The side we can see here is the side that was facing the Sun at that time.

Five inner planets

Astronomers also thought that another planet orbited the Sun, closer than Mercury. Some people even thought they saw it. They called it **Vulcan**. Now we know that there are no other planets inside Mercury's orbit. So, there are just four inner planets.

Scientists use huge radiotelescopes, like this one in Puerto Rico, to study the planets in our solar system.

What is Mercury like?

Mercury is the smallest of the **inner planets**. It is so small that it is very difficult to see it from Earth. Even using the largest telescopes on Earth, Mercury still looks like a small dot. It is also very difficult to send **spaceprobes** there. This is because the Sun is so large that it makes a huge amount of **gravity** and pulls spacecraft off-course. That makes controlling a spacecraft very difficult.

Covered in craters

Mercury looks quite like the **Moon**. They are about the same size, and both of them are covered with round holes. These are called **craters**. They are made when **asteroids** hit the planet and blow up. Mercury has some enormous craters. One of these is called the Caloris Basin. It is 1300 kilometres wide. It must have been made when a very big asteroid hit Mercury.

Scientists used this image of Mercury to discover what materials make up the planet's crust.

Some craters have bright, straight lines pointing away from them. These are called rays. They are rocks that were blown out of the crater when it formed.

There are also some very large cliffs on Mercury. They are called **scarps** and can be up to 3 kilometres high. **Astronomers** have named the scarps after famous explorers' ships on Earth.

No atmosphere

An **atmosphere** is a layer of gas surrounding a planet. Most planets have an atmosphere, but Mercury is so small that it does not. This is because it does not make enough gravity to hold onto any gas. So there are no clouds, no wind and no rain on Mercury.

There are smooth hills and domes between the scarps, or cliffs, in the Caloris Basin.

Slowly spinning planet

Mercury takes 59 Earth days to spin around once. Billions of years ago, Mercury probably spun around much faster. The gravity of the Sun has slowed it down. Most planets follow circles around the Sun, but Mercury travels in an oval. Its **orbit** is also tilted upwards a little. Sometimes we can see Mercury passing right in front of the Sun. When this happens, it is called a **transit**. It is very dangerous to look straight at the Sun – never do it, even with sunglasses. It can damage your eyes. So, astronomers use special telescopes to watch it happen. Mercury looks like a tiny black spot travelling across the face of the Sun. The first time this was seen to happen was in 1631.

Because Mercury has no atmosphere to protect it, the surface is always either extremely hot or extremely cold.

Hot and cold

Because Mercury turns so slowly, the Sun stays in the sky for a long time. The Sun appears very large in Mercury's sky because it is so close to the planet. During the daytime, the temperature on Mercury can rise to above 350° Celsius; about as hot as the hotplate on a kitchen cooker can become. This is hot enough to melt some metals. When it is night on Mercury, it becomes very cold. The temperature can fall to –170° Celsius. On Earth the coldest temperature ever recorded was –89.2° Celsius. It was measured in Antarctica on 21 July 1983.

How many spacecraft have travelled to Mercury?

Only one spacecraft has ever flown close to Mercury. It was an American **spaceprobe** called *Mariner 10*. It travelled to Mercury in 1974 and 1975. *Mariner 10* flew past Mercury three times. It took thousands of pictures of the planet. Unfortunately, all of them were of the same side of the planet. So, astronomers have only ever seen one half of Mercury.

Now scientists have developed a new kind of rocket engine, called an **ion engine**. Spacecraft with ion engines will be able to fly close to Mercury. Scientists in Europe and the USA are now building new spacecraft to go to Mercury.

Mariner 10 *was launched in November 1973.*

What is Venus like?

Venus is about the same size as Earth. Some **astronomers** call it Earth's sister. Venus comes closer to Earth than any other **planet**. When the two planets are at their closest, they are 45 million kilometres apart. That is very close in space! The Sun is 150 million kilometres from Earth.

It's hot!

The **atmosphere** of Venus is made of a gas called **carbon dioxide**. The planet is wrapped in blankets of thick cloud. There is never a clear day on Venus. The clouds keep the planet warm. It is a bit like the way a greenhouse keeps plants warm in a garden. Scientists call the way clouds keep a planet warm the 'greenhouse effect'. The clouds heat Venus to over 450° Celsius. That is about twice as hot as a kitchen oven.

*Venus is named after the ancient Roman goddess of beauty. Wrapped in clouds Venus looks similar to Earth, but we could not survive there. There is no **oxygen** for us to breathe and no water to drink.*

Acid rain

The clouds on Venus are not like the clouds we have on Earth. On Earth, the clouds are made of **water vapour**. On Venus, the clouds are made of deadly chemicals. When it rains on Venus, it rains **sulfuric acid**. This acid can eat through metal.

Volcanoes on Venus

There are many mountains on Venus and scientists think that some might be **volcanoes**. They do not know if they are **extinct** or still **erupting**. There is a lot of lightning on Venus. Most of it happens in one spot – a place called Beta Regio. There are mountains in Beta Regio that astronomers think look like volcanoes. On Earth, there is often lightning near a volcano just before it erupts. Some scientists think the lightning on Venus means that the volcanoes are still erupting.

What is the tallest mountain on Venus?

The tallest mountain on Venus is called Mount Maxwell. The mountain is 11 kilometres high. That is 2 kilometres higher than Mount Everest, the highest mountain on Earth.

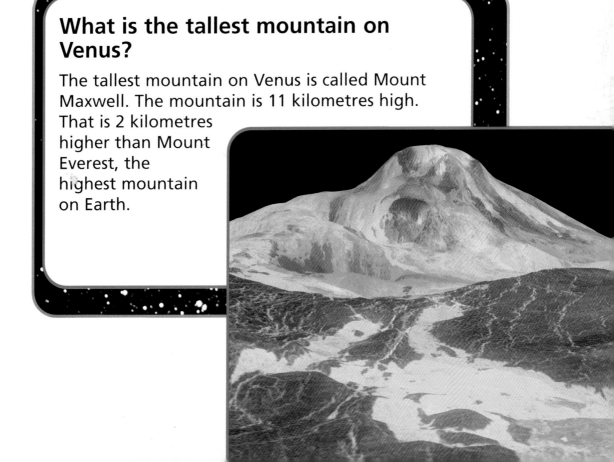

Counting craters

Scientists can count the **craters** on a planet to tell how old the surface is. The more craters there are, the older the surface is. There are not many craters on Venus. The whole surface of the planet appears to be only about 500 million years old.

Astronomers believe that all the planets in our solar system formed at the same time as the Sun. That was 4.5 billion years ago. So the surface of Venus is quite young. Some scientists believe that every 500 million years, all of the volcanoes on Venus erupt at once. This would cover the entire planet in red-hot **lava**. It would totally destroy everything that was there before and create a new surface on the planet.

This picture of the surface of Venus is colour-coded to show the high and low points.

Who has sent spaceprobes to Venus?

During the 1970s, the Russians and the Americans sent **spaceprobes** to Venus. Most of them travelled around the planet, looking down at the clouds. Some used **radar**, to look at the surface of the planet. A radar sends **radio waves** to the planet and measures how long it takes for the waves to bounce back. Using this information, scientists can make a picture of the planet's surface. Some of the Russian spaceprobes landed on the surface of Venus. This is how we know the surface is so dangerous. It was so hot that each spaceprobe only worked for about an hour, and only sent back a few pictures. The heat on Venus destroyed the spaceprobes. The clouds on Venus block out a lot of the sunlight. Pictures from the Russian spacecraft show that the clouds turn the sunlight orange.

This is an artist's drawing of Mariner 2, *which went to Venus after* Mariner 1 *was destroyed by a launch failure.*

Why is Mars red?

Mars is a desert **planet**. There is very little water there today. It was not always like this. Mars was once like Earth. It had rivers, and it may even have had an ocean. Pictures of Mars have been sent back to Earth by **spaceprobes**. They show the way water has cut into the rocks on Mars.

Rusty planet!

There are no rivers or oceans on Mars today. Most of the water has gone. Powerful light from the Sun, called **ultraviolet light** can break up water. On Earth, our water is protected from the Sun by a special layer of **oxygen** in our **atmosphere**, called the **ozone layer**. Mars has no ozone layer. When water breaks up, it makes two gases. One kind of gas is called **hydrogen**. The other gas is called oxygen.

When this happened on Mars, the hydrogen gas floated off into space. Oxygen is heavier than hydrogen, and the **gravity** of Mars pulled the oxygen to the ground. The oxygen joined to the rocks on the ground. The rocks contain a metal called iron. When iron joins with oxygen, it turns red. We call this rust. The whole surface of Mars has gone rusty.

Mars looks rocky and dry. Scientists have not found any signs of life there.

In 1997, the USA landed a small robot on Mars. It was called *Sojourner*. It drove across the surface looking at the rocks. It sent back valuable information to scientists here on Earth.

There are four very large **volcanoes** on Mars. They are no longer erupting and scientists say that they are extinct.

Mount Olympus, on Mars, is the tallest volcano in our solar system. This photo shows what Mount Olympus looks like from 900 kilometres (560 miles) above the surface.

Is the water underground?

Some scientists think that there may still be lakes of water buried under the ground on Mars. A new spaceprobe is being built in Europe. It is called *Mars Express*, and it will look for underground lakes using **radar**.

Is there life on Mars?

Many people have thought there is life on Mars. In 1877, Mars passed close to Earth and many **astronomers** watched it through their **telescopes**. Some thought they saw straight lines on the **planet**. They wondered if these were like man-made rivers, called canals, but built by **Martians**. Scientists made bigger telescopes to see the canals more clearly. When they looked at Mars through the bigger telescopes, the canals had disappeared. The lines had been caused by faults in the earlier telescopes!

Powerful telescopes are needed to see even the largest canyons on the surface of Mars.

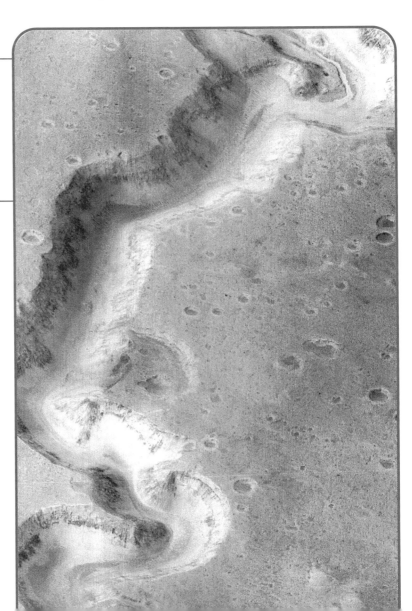

Microscopic life

Now spacecraft have photographed all of Mars. There are no cities or roads on the planet. There has never been intelligent life on Mars. Many scientists think that very simple **microscopic** life might have lived on the planet billions of years ago, when Mars had lots of water.

Some scientists think that there may still be microscopic life living below the surface of Mars. They would live where there is water. Another place to look would be at the North and South **Poles** of Mars. There is still some water there, but it is frozen into ice.

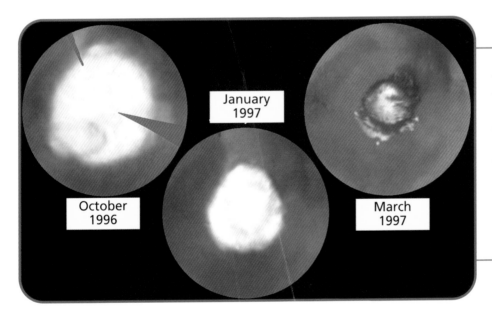

January 1997

October 1996

March 1997

Scientists have studied how the size of the northern polar cap on Mars changes over time.

Water on the planets

All life needs water. There is no water on the other two inner planets. **Mercury** has never had water. If there had been water on Mercury, the **craters** would have been washed away. It is almost certain that there has never been life of any kind on Mercury. **Venus** may have had water billions of years ago. Now it is so hot that all the water has drifted off into space. So there can be no life on Venus.

What is inside the inner planets?

All of the **inner planets** are round balls of rock and metal. There are different amounts of rocks and metal in each planet. The metals are heavy and mostly found in the centre of the planet. This is called the core. Lighter rocks sit on top of the core. This is called the mantle. The very top layer of rocks makes up the surface of the planet. This layer is called the crust. It is very thin compared to the mantle and core.

Studying orbits

Scientists can work out the size of a planet's core, mantle and crust by studying the way spacecraft **orbit** around the planet. When a spacecraft travels around a planet, it is pulled by the planet's **gravity**. Metals make more gravity than rock. Scientists can work out how much rock and metal is inside a planet by the amount a spacecraft is pulled towards it.

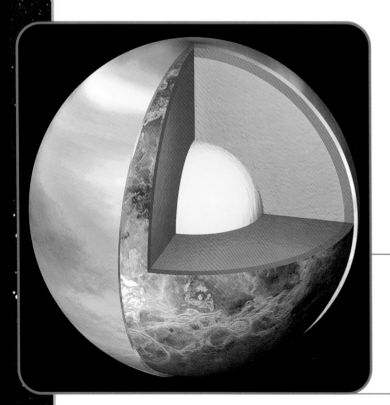

This picture has cut away sections. It shows the different sizes of the layers of Venus.

A planet's core

Mercury is the smallest inner planet but it has a large core. Mercury's core takes up almost as much space as its mantle. On Venus and Mars the mantle takes up ten times more space than the core. Scientists still do not know why Mercury has such a large core.

The core of a planet can be a **magnet**. Earth's core is quite a strong magnet. The other inner planets are all much weaker. Rocks in the mantle can be so hot that they become runny. They are said to be **molten**. If they find their way up through cracks in the crust they can **erupt** onto the surface of the planet and make **volcanoes**.

This photograph shows a close-up view of the Discovery Rupes *scarp* on Mercury.

Could we ever live on Mars?

Scientists in the USA, Russia and Europe are all interested in sending humans to Mars. Many plans have been made. Humans who go into space are called **astronauts**. It will be very difficult to send humans to Mars. It would not be like sending astronauts to the **Moon**, because Mars is much further away. It only takes three days for a spacecraft to get to the Moon. It takes nine months to travel the hundreds of millions of kilometres from Earth to Mars.

Space travel

It costs a lot of money to travel through space. To go to Mars would need a very big spacecraft to carry enough fuel and food to keep the astronauts alive. So, it would be very expensive. At the moment it would cost too much to send astronauts to Mars. Scientists must find ways to make the spacecraft smaller and less expensive. One way to do this would be to make the rocket fuel for the journey home, from chemicals found on Mars. Another way would be to grow food on the spacecraft.

Viking I *was launched from Cape Canaveral, USA, and began its orbit around Mars in 1976.*

Making rocket fuel

Scientists have worked out how to make rocket fuel on Mars. They would first send a small spacecraft to Mars without any humans on it. It would land on Mars and begin to make rocket fuel. When it had made enough fuel, humans would set off from Earth. They would grow food on their spacecraft in special greenhouses, and eat this during their journey.

The astronauts would land on Mars, next to the first spacecraft. They would probably stay on Mars for a year and explore the **planet**. When it was time to return home, they would use the rocket fuel made by the first spacecraft to blast off from Mars. The journey home to Earth would take another nine months.

The Pathfinder *mission sent back views of Mars like this one.*

Living on Mars will be difficult. The planet has a very thin **atmosphere** and is made of a gas that humans cannot breathe. So **astronauts** on Mars would have to wear spacesuits any time they wanted to walk around or explore outside. They would only be able to take off the spacesuits inside their spacecraft.

The image on the right shows how completely a dust storm once covered Mars. The details of the planet, which we can see on the left, are completely hidden by the storm.

Brave explorers

Every spring, enormous dust storms cover the surface of Mars. These would be dangerous for the astronauts. They will be very far away from home for a very long time. One of the astronauts would have to be a doctor, in case any of the other astronauts became ill or was hurt.

Even though it would be dangerous, there are many reasons for going to Mars. It is the planet most like Earth. It will be impossible to explore the whole planet with robots. Humans are much better at exploring than robots.

Sojourner *was a robot sent to Mars in 1997. It was part of the* Pathfinder *mission, and sent back coloured pictures from the surface of Mars.*

A world just like ours

Some scientists even think that humans could build factories to make air on Mars. They could also plant trees on the planet. It would take a lot of money to do this. It would also take hundreds of years for the planet to change. If it worked, humans in the future would be able to walk around on Mars without spacesuits. Mars could become a world just like Earth.

Fact file

Earth

Time to spin once: 24 hours.
Size: 12,750 kilometres (7922 miles) across
Distance from Sun: 150 million kilometres
Time to go around the Sun: 365.25 days (So every fourth year we have to include an extra day in the calendar, February 29th. These are known as leap years. If we did not do this, the seasons would shift out of order with the months of the year.)
Surface area: 510 million square kilometres
Average temperature: 20° Celsius
Number of Moons: 1

Mercury

Time to spin once: 59 days
Size: 4878 kilometres across
Distance from the Sun: Between 70 million and 46 million kilometres (Mercury has an oval orbit).
Time to go around the Sun: 88 days
Surface area: 7.5 million square kilometres
Average temperature: 350° Celsius
Gravity (compared to Earth):   38 per cent
Number of moons: 0

When images of Earth and Mars are placed next to each other, we can see that Earth is much larger.

Venus

Time to spin once: 243 days
Size: 12,104 kilometres across
Distance from the Sun:
   108 million kilometres
Time to go around the Sun: 225 days
Surface area: 460 million square kilometres
Average temperature: 460° Celsius
Gravity (compared to Earth):   90 per cent
Number of moons: 0

Mars

Time to spin once:
   24 hours 37mins
Size: 6794 kilometres across
Distance from the Sun:
   228 million kilometres
Time to go around the Sun:
   687 days
Surface area: 140 million
   square kilometres
Average temperature:
   –23° Celsius
Gravity (compared to Earth):
   38 per cent
Number of moons: 2

An artist's idea of what asteroids look like, floating through space. Many of the planets, including Earth, have huge craters from asteroids crashing into their surfaces.

Glossary

asteroid small object orbiting the Sun – some are just lumps of rock floating in space

astronauts people who travel and work in space

astronomers scientists who study space, planets and stars

atmosphere layer of gases that cover a planet

axis imaginary line through a planet, from North to South Pole, around which it spins

carbon dioxide one of the common gases in the universe

celestial police group of astronomers in 1800, who searched for a planet between Mars and Jupiter

constellation pattern of stars in the sky – each constellation has a name

crater hole on the surface of a planet or moon

Deimos smaller of the two moons that orbit Mars

erupt burst or force out violently

extinct something that will never come to life or become active again

gravity force that pulls all objects towards the surface of Earth, or any other planet, moon or star

hydrogen most common gas in the universe

inner planets the four planets closest to the Sun – Mercury, Venus, Earth and Mars

ion engine new kind of engine for a spacecraft

lava molten rock that erupts out of volcanoes

magnet something that attracts anything made of iron

Martians beings who were thought to live on Mars

microscopic very tiny – it can only be seen through a microscope

molten rocks that are so hot they are runny

moon small object that orbits a planet

Moon, the small, rocky object that orbits Earth. Astronauts first landed on the Moon in 1969.

Mount Maxwell largest mountain on Venus

orbit path one object in space takes around another

outer planets the five planets furthest from the Sun – Jupiter, Saturn, Uranus, Neptune and Pluto

oxygen gas humans need to breathe

ozone layer protective layer of gases in our atmosphere

Phobos larger of the two moons that orbit Mars

planet large object that orbits a star. Earth is a planet.

Pole one end of the axis around which a planet spins

radar special radio used to look through clouds and some rocks

radio wave electromagnetic wave that carries sounds or pictures through the air

scarp large cliff

spaceprobe spacecraft that sends back information to Earth from space

sulfuric acid thick, colourless, oily liquid. It is a dangerous acid, made from sulfur.

telescope device with one lens to look through that makes objects seem larger and nearer

transit when a planet passes in front of the Sun

ultraviolet light very powerful part of the Sun's light

volcano opening in a planet's surface through which hot liquid rock is thrown up

Vulcan planet once thought to be between Mercury and the Sun. It does not exist.

water vapour gas, like mist, that water turns into when it is heated

Further reading

Exploring the Solar System: Mercury, Giles Sparrow (Heinemann Library, 2001)

Exploring the Solar System: Mars, Giles Sparrow (Heinemann Library, 2001)

Exploring the Solar System: Venus, Giles Sparrow (Heinemann Library, 2001)

How the universe works, Heather Couper and Nigel Henbest (Dorling Kindersley, 1999)

Index